CONNECTIONS THAT COUNT

A STRAIGHT-TALK GUIDE

BY SCOTT OLDFORD

TABLE OF CONTENTS

Scott Oldford is living this! If you want to learn how to make connections matter for your business and your life overall, you'll want to absorb this book and take action!

Chris Brogan, *author of*
The Freaks Shall Inherit the Earth

WHY EMAIL MAKES ME SWEATY

I clicked *send* and promptly broke out in a sweat. But I couldn't take it back. I couldn't take any of it back. The dinner invitation was already in their inbox. They didn't know me. I didn't know them. And still, I was inviting them to dinner. Quite possibly, they had already opened the email invitation.

And probably deleted it.

Probably.

I couldn't have known then that email would change my life and the way I do business. I'll confess, even now—almost 100 dinners and lunches, 700 strangers-turned-friends, and way too many steak dinners later—clicking *send* still makes me nervous.

There's the possibility of being rejected, of feeling like a fool. And that's before the actual dinner happens. So many missteps can be taken during dinner. If I think about it too much, it makes me wonder why I continue hosting these meals. Stepping outside of my comfort zone—no matter how many times—is tough to do.

But it is worth it.

And I remember my "why" every time I host another dinner. Every time I walk into a restaurant and wait for a new group of strangers—and soon-to-be friends, colleagues, and possible business partners—that surge of adrenaline reminds me. These meals are about making connections, hearing new ideas, solving problems, seeing the world from other people's perspectives. Everything fades into the background as guests—from all walks of life and from all different industries—introduce themselves, talk about their struggles and obstacles, and ask questions of the rest of the group. There is laughter. There is a buzz of excitement when someone offers a new idea. There are quiet moments when someone shares something profoundly personal. There are connections that continue long after the dinner is over.

Bluntly put, every dinner is worth the planning, nerves, and time put into making sure it goes off without a hitch. It's something that I think everyone should do. It's changed my life and the way I do business, and I know you'll be changed by it, too.

I'll be honest: the first time you decide to invite strangers to a group lunch or dinner, you are going to freak out. You'll want to cancel. (You'll try to convince yourself that maybe, just maybe, you should.)

But if you're like me—which, if you're reading this, you probably are—you don't mind temporary discomfort. You know that the best opportunities and experiences in life begin with stretching and challenging yourself. And you're ready to do that.

That's how I found myself clicking *send* on that very first email. I knew something was missing in the way I did business—and it had to do with connecting with others. As an entrepreneur, I had been networked to death. I was tired of business cards and elevator pitches. I was tired of meaningless connections that meant nothing the minute I left. I was tired of stilted conversations that made me want to fall asleep standing up.

Something needed to change. I needed to change. I found the solution: I began sharing my dinner with others. I began hosting Limitless Dinners and Lunches. In the past six months—at the time of writing this—I've hosted them across North America and have invited everyone from struggling artists to billionaires, from social media experts to journalists.

"SOMETHING NEEDED TO CHANGE. I NEEDED TO CHANGE."

These shared meals have expanded my circle and created a network of forward-thinkers that is webbed across Canada and the United States. I've found my tribe in Limitless Dinners and Lunches, and it's allowed me to connect to and learn from some of the most brilliant people in the world. But it's not just about what this strategy provides for me.

At Limitless Dinners and Lunches, I've seen 19 (known) business deals happen for other people. I've seen partnerships form. I've seen someone receive $250,000 in funding. I've seen friendships begin. I've seen meaningful relationships start from sitting elbow to elbow and sharing dinner and dessert.

It seems random ... but it's not a mistake. When I bring people together for conversations, connections are created that I've never found anywhere else.

So, are you ready? For relationship-building? To stretch yourself and your conversation skills? To send that first email to a stranger?

Before we jump in, here are a few ground rules:

- This isn't a numbers game. Though I've done 80 of these so far, I've strived for quality—not quantity.
- Bringing people together and bringing the right people together are not synonymous. It's the difference between networking and connecting.
- Expect the unexpected. These lunches and dinners have a power and life of their own—don't set time limits.
- This isn't about you. It's about ensuring that everyone at the table leaves with more knowledge and more understanding than when they arrived.
- You can't invite everyone to dinner. Some people aren't ready or willing to engage in these kinds of conversations. And that's okay.
- Egos need to be checked at the door. 'Nuff said.
- These conversations are meant to be deep. If you're engaging in small talk, you're doing it wrong.
- These lunches and dinners are curated. You need to be intentional in how and why you bring people together.
- As much as you may want to scale lunches and dinners, they don't scale well. You can't scale intimacy.

Got it? Good. Let's get started.

HOW THE SAUSAGE GETS MADE

When it comes to creating these focused dinners, you have one job. It's not to secure funding for your next idea. It's not to drive revenue to your business. It's not about finding someone who can help you with your book deal. Or who can suggest a designer for your new website.

Repeat after me: *It's not about me.*

It's about relationships. You want to create relationships that will last, relationships that will move people forward in their goals. That's it. That's your job. And believe me, it's much harder than it seems. (But it can be done!)

> **"REPEAT AFTER ME: *IT'S NOT* ABOUT ME."**

I've developed a simple method to achieve success in connecting with like-minded people. It's not difficult. It's not rocket science. And while it takes dedication, you can do it.

PICK YOUR MOTIVE

Your motive for the lunch or dinner is not only important but it's also the difference between networking and connecting. The motive is important: it's the common thread and will keep conversations flowing, allowing you to get past small talk about the weather and today's headlines. No one actually cares about those conversations. You want to go beyond. You want each person to leave and have a new perspective, a new challenge, a new friend.

> ***"...WHILE FACILITATING A LUNCH OR DINNER, YOU ARE TRYING TO MOVE EVERYONE TO ONE COMMON GOAL."***

If you're hosting a dinner with only people from the same industry, would you invite just one person outside of it? That person is going to have a difficult time connecting, aren't they? This doesn't mean that everyone at the table needs to be in the same industry or at the same level in business. What it does mean is that, while facilitating a lunch or dinner, you are trying to move everyone to one common goal.

For me, it's about helping people overcome their challenges. Obstacles and challenges are unifying because everyone has them. Everyone experiences them and can offer suggestions and solutions for others encountering similar situations.

You have two choices when obstacles are presented: use them as a catapult to greatness or use them as road blocks. These choices are the crux of our conversations. That's where the magic happens.

I got to know Scott after he invited me to an interview on his podcast, and we had a wide ranging discussion, about everything but insurance. Later he invited me to lunch and subsequently to that, dinner. I had no idea who else would be attending and not being a "natural networker", I attended but with some trepidation. What was the purpose of inviting me? Was this just an attempt to sell me something?

Once I attended, it was anything but a sales pitch. Just a few people, some of who I had lots in common with, and some I had never met before, talking about business issues and challenges. I learned a lot, made some great connections and enjoyed hearing how many of us have the same challenges whether or not we are independent entrepreneurs, large business leaders, managers, or executives. Best of all, it flowed really naturally and never felt like "networking" which is something I avoid like the plague.

Read Scott's book, and see if you have the courage to create your own version of the "Limitless Dinner".

Tom Hickey

UNDERSTAND YOUR VALUE

Your reason for lunch or dinner is to facilitate the transfer of knowledge, not to talk about yourself. It's not about showing how great you are for having brought people together. It's not about boosting your business. It's about asking the right questions and connecting people at that table to ensure that the conversation is as smooth as possible.

The lunch and dinner that you host has to be filled with meaningful conversations or it's pointless. Your job is to create an equal playing field between the dominant and meeker personalities in the room.

Your purpose for hosting the party is to squeeze every last minute out of the time together. You're intent on making sure that everyone has the opportunity to learn and share—that everyone gets as much as they give.

The problem: the host may feel intimidated and get nervous. (You've probably seen this happen at an event; perhaps you've even felt that way!) People who feel intimidated and nervous forget what they're trying to do with that event. They feel self-conscious. They think that their purpose isn't good enough for the guests. Even though they never voice it, the way they host the event speaks loudly. They let the event control itself instead of controlling the event. Time gets wasted. People become bored or feel left out. People begin checking their phones and watches. The purpose of the event gets lost—even if the original purpose was fantastic.

The lesson is simple: be confident in what you've promised your guests. The meal will be great, the conversation will be sparkling, and your guests will love it. You have to believe it first.

"... BE CONFIDENT IN WHAT YOU'VE PROMISED YOUR GUESTS."

PICK YOUR GUESTS

When you start hosting lunches and dinners, you will get resistance. It happens because change makes people nervous. They're afraid of "what if" instead of "what could be." This means that when you're looking for the right people, it's important to look for common traits that show that they are forward-thinking and the right fit for your meal.

"I'LL BE HONEST: IF YOU'RE LOOKING SOLELY FOR A MONETARY VALUE TO THIS ACTIVITY, YOU MIGHT NOT GET IT."

People sometimes have difficulty wrapping their minds around having dinner with strangers. They are critical of how it could actually provide value, how they'll "get" something out of it. I'll be honest: if you're looking solely for a monetary value to this activity, you might not get it. (Then again, I've seen many business deals and funding agreements made around the table.) But a tangible, monetary value is not what these meals are about. It's about finding people who are thinkers and doers. You want to find people who are interesting, who have something to share, and who can broaden your worldview. You want to be around and learn from forward-thinking people. Make sure that you invite people like that.

MAKE IT A LEARNING EXPERIENCE FOR EVERYONE

The last thing you want to do is invite the wrong person. Trust me. Early on, I hosted a dinner with all senior business types, all who had over 25 years of experience. With that group, I mistakenly invited someone who had little experience in the industry. From the beginning, it was obvious that I had made a mistake; they were not a good fit for that particular dinner setting. After they arrived 30 minutes late, the conversation went from being fun, exciting, and authentic to a moderated, stuffy discussion. Later I realized that the dinner would have gone much more smoothly had I invited multiple junior people as well.

The lesson? Your invitations should go to a mixture of people with similar experiences. In this way, each person can learn and mentor the other, allowing for everyone to add and take value and leave the lunch or dinner satisfied. People generally love learning and mentoring. By mixing experience levels, everyone can accomplish two valuable goals: knowledge transfer and connection creation.

"YOUR INVITATIONS SHOULD GO TO A MIXTURE OF PEOPLE WITH SIMILAR EXPERIENCES."

As you grow your connections, you might want to invite through The Bucket Method. Those you surround yourself with are in one of three buckets: those who are one step behind you, one in front of you, and in the same place as you. By inviting people from each bucket, you can achieve three things: mentor those behind you, learn from those ahead of you, and discuss challenges with those who are going through what you are. By splitting your guests into thirds, you add value to and take value from all guests.

USE YOUR CONNECTIONS

I planned a trip to New York earlier this year. As I didn't know many people in New York, I reached out to a few friends—including Chris Brogan. I knew that he was well connected and he knows I don't sales-pitch.

Chris Brogan filled half of my 14-person dinner with absolutely amazing people. I'm talking authors, Forbes writers, top real-estate agents, and everyone in between. This allowed me to start from a position of advantage and focus on inviting people like Gary Vaynerchuk to dinner.

While it's not your goal to have "celebs" at your lunches and dinners, having people introduce you to others allows you to pick the correct people for that particular meal and ensure that it brings incredible insight to those present.

Remember: this doesn't always work well and, if you host meals frequently, you can't go back and ask your friends for new connections every week. But if you plan and ask at the right time, every person has a wealth of interesting connections. People usually introduce you to people whom they trust, which means you get their top tier of relationships. That's valuable!

"PEOPLE USUALLY INTRODUCE YOU TO PEOPLE WHOM THEY TRUST, WHICH MEANS YOU GET THEIR TOP TIER OF RELATIONSHIPS."

Patience is crucial at this stage. If you're looking to invite someone to lunch or dinner, don't blast six people at the same time. Being patient allows you to put together your lunch or dinner, knowing that you've invited the right people for the situation. The last thing you want to do is to invite someone twice or have the wrong people at the table.

USE THE INTERNET

Did you know that there's a website with more than 40,000 professionals available for a phone call from you? It'll cost you a few bucks a minute ... but damn, it's powerful. The website Clarity.FM is the perfect place to find new guests for your next meal.

"...DAMN, IT'S POWERFUL."

And here's the best part—you don't even have to call them and spend the minute-by-minute fee. You can contact any of the Clarity.FM members for absolutely free. Just search by location and then narrow down your results from there.

You can also do this with other social media sites. LinkedIn has a powerful search tool and with the right connections it's simple to get introduced to others. Facebook offers a search function by location—just key in "People I know in [location]" or "People I may know in [location]." Since you can directly message people on Facebook even if you're not their friend, there are fewer hoops to jump through. And then there's Twitter. I hate Twitter, but if you use Twitter's search, you can also locate possible guests by specific professions and specific places. This does take a little more time on the front end, but it's easy to tweet out to others and get a response quickly.

You can also use your own social network by emailing your friends and other connections for suggestions for the invitation list. If you're part of our Limitless Business Facebook group—an exclusive curated group for thinkers and entrepreneurs—you can always post your location and ask for suggestions or if anyone would be interested in attending. (By the way, if you're not part of the Limitless Business group, send me an email. We're always looking for new members!)

This is the book I wish I read when I started building my business and realized I needed to develop a great network. I had heard a million times, "its not what you know, it's who you know" but had no clue how to develop meaningful relationships with people who could help me (or people who I could help, for that matter). Connections that Count fixes that problem. The author explains how to find great people, how to invite them out, how to connect with them, how to followup with them, and even how to combat your nerves if you have a bit of anxiety about talking to strangers, which I do. Regardless of where you are in the ongoing process of building your network, but this book. I'm confident you'll be glad you did. It's added numerous rich relationships to my life.

Jason Connell, *Founder Ignited Leadership*

PICK THE VENUE

Location, location, location. After choosing your guests, the next most important thing about your dinner or lunch is the location. At the risk of sounding like a snob, I'll say that the choice of a unique restaurant is always an ace in your back pocket—delicious food and an interesting ambiance are always intriguing and impressive.

Typically, I develop relationships with the management and owners of one or two restaurants in a particular location. In turn, I can expand or retract the size of the lunch or dinner on a moment's notice and take advantage of the private room—without the hefty minimum needed for most venues.

No matter where you decide to have your meal, remember that private rooms are where it's at. I didn't use a private room until about three months after I began hosting dinners. Seriously. It's a game-changer.

> ***"SERIOUSLY. IT'S A GAME-CHANGER."***

While you may not be able to do this at the beginning as many places require a minimum cost for each person, private rooms give the space and quietness needed to create the right atmosphere for people to open up and participate in the most meaningful conversations.

PLAN THE DINNER

By far the most time-consuming and difficult part of holding lunches and dinners is organizing the events. When I started, it was pretty "old-school." It took an enormous amount of planning and memory to remember what was what. But, like everything, familiarity breeds comfort, and after several dinners, I started innovating.

While the system I use isn't flawless, and there isn't a doubt in my mind that you can improve upon this system, it's cut the amount of planning time to at least a fourth of my original time.

"BUT, LIKE EVERYTHING, FAMILIARITY BREEDS COMFORT, AND AFTER SEVERAL DINNERS, I STARTED INNOVATING."

After receiving the initial reply from a guest ("Yes, Scott! I'd love to attend your dinner!"), I send another email that asks that guest to select his or her availability using TypeForm. While this is a little impersonal, it allows me to collect information and organize the event easier and faster than tracking it in an Excel sheet. It also gives the person that you invited more control over which dates and times work for his or her specific calendar.

After they've confirmed a date and time, TypeForm notifies me with an email saying they've confirmed. Now the fun starts.

Using TypeForm, I collect the information of the guests that I've invited. After the "deadline" that I've set, I transfer the information into an Excel sheet. Doing so allows me to sort people both by availability and who should meet who based on their professions and their biggest challenges (which they've listed in TypeForm). It sounds a little Machiavellian, but if you can make chemistry happen faster, why wouldn't you?

Then it's on to the next step of the process: the follow-up.

The guests have all given me a bunch of different times, so I follow up to ensure that the time I have chosen works for them. I typically do this with the use of Contactually. Not only does it let me import them to my CRM but it also allows me to send one email to 10 people at the same time, customized with their individual names.

After I receive confirmation, I turn their cells green and add them to the Google Calendar invite so that it will automatically remind them before the event. Keep in mind, I keep the entire guest list secret until they arrive. If you'd like to do it that way, be sure to check the box "Keep guest list private."

We've just made it through the hardest part! The rest is just setting up an automated program in Contactually that does the following items:

1) Reminds guests three days before the event.

2) Reminds guests the day before the event.

3) Reminds guests the morning of the event.

4) Connects all guests the day after the event.

Keep in mind that there will be plenty of changes—people will cancel, be late, and everything in between. This is difficult to manage so I usually employ Fancy Hands to take care of those changes for me. I always include an email address that guests can use for any delays or cancellations so that I can ensure that we update the restaurant. Fancy Hands receives these emails and works with that person to ensure they are either re-booked for another lunch or calls the restaurant to ensure that there is time to re-book the table.

PREPARATION THE DAY OF THE DINNER

The day of your event is a big day. Treat it as such. Arrive at least 30 minutes prior to the event's beginning so that you're comfortable and not flustered. You don't want to be stuck in traffic wondering if you'll make it on time ... or worse, be the last person to the meal you've organized.

During those 30 minutes, you'll want to talk to the restaurant's host so that he or she understands the purpose of your lunch or dinner. You'll want to ask the host to interrupt as little as possible. You'll also want to ask him or her to allow the end of the meal to be as organic as possible, rather than rushing the bill and bringing it out before the group has finished.

You'll also want to be available prior to the dinner to field any phone calls from lost guests and to welcome your guests.

At the beginning of the meal, ask everyone to turn off and put away their phones so that they will be fully present in this experience. Nothing kills a conversation as quickly as people preoccupied with their buzzing, blinking phones rather than the sparkling topics at hand.

FACILITATING THE MEAL

Great! A bunch of people have arrived for lunch or dinner—now you can sit back and relax.

Just kidding.

This is where you either succeed or fail. This is the point where you either make or break the lunch or dinner. It's your go-time. You've done way too much planning to let it go now.

> ***"THIS IS WHERE YOU EITHER SUCCEED OR FAIL."***

In my experience, lunches or dinners that have no format and no facilitation are useless. Without guidance, thought, methodology, or intention, the lunch or dinner becomes whatever it becomes. If you are hosting certain lunches or dinners, their format-lessness can work, but for the purpose of fostering connections and creating opportunities for all guests, not so much.

Here's how I keep conversations focused and moving:

Four Guests and Under

Sometimes a few people cancel moments before the event. While these people had better have a good reason or are "un-friended" for cancelling on the day of the event, it does happen and, when it does, it can swing the lunch or dinner into Awkward Land.

In this situation, the conversation will be random. I know it goes against my first rule—to have structure—but it's tough (and a little too much like an interview) to have a heavily structured conversation with such a small group. The best way to deal with such a small group is to engage with each other and connect with each other's biggest challenges. Let the conversation happen.

As you can probably tell, I'm not a big fan of such small get-togethers. I find that they create a little awkwardness—the conversation usually

Breaking bread, breaking obstacles, opening minds, opening perspectives, sharing truths, Sharing wine. The first 15 minutes different, The next 90 minutes magic. This isn't on any express menu anywhere. Good things brewing.

Kevin Casey

ends early. A few months ago, I planned a lunch for eight people in Toronto. For whatever reason, only four of us ended up at The Keg. It was the first time that I had hosted such a small group, although I had expected a larger one. Although the conversation was effective, and two of the guests became business partners, it can certainly blindside the facilitator.

Six to Eight

Six is the best format for a lunch event. For dinner, it's eight. Here's why: with six people you can have a specific method, while still ensuring that everyone is having the same conversation. It also allows you to talk about each set of challenges and problems and give advice for a solid 15 minutes each. This offers incredible knowledge-transfer and allows guests to connect instead of network with each other.

Here is the typical format that I use with lunches or dinners of this size:

1) Allow all guests to engage in small talk but don't introduce anyone except by their name. As you know everyone—but your guests probably don't—you can guide the discussion better than anyone there.

2) Once menus have been distributed, try to guide the group in the direction of actually ordering food. Usually groups have a difficult time doing that as they are more concerned with the conversation than what they'll eat. But remember—meaningful conversation can't happen until food orders have been placed.

3) After the last person has ordered, it's all you. Thank everyone for being there and then present the format for the get-together.

Here's what I typically say:

Thanks so much for being here today! It's not every day that I get to spend lunch with such brilliant people. Since I've started bringing people together in this fashion, I like to add a little structure so that we have time to help each other with our obstacles and have the ability to truly connect with each other.

In order to do this, I'd like to go around the table. When we get to you, talk about three specific things: first, who you are and what you're passionate about right now; second, what's keeping you awake at night, or your greatest challenge and how it could be solved; and third, a random question for the table (or yourself).

I select a person whom I know best. I can guide that person in the direction of the best format for the lunch or dinner compared to its becoming whatever he or she wants it to be.

By now you're thinking, *Well, that's great, but it's only going to take 20 minutes.* Believe it or not, it typically takes at least an hour (at best) to get through six introductions. The magic of this approach is that guests start discussing, offering advice, and talking as a group.

Typically you'll need to keep the conversation on track and ask the questions. You'll also need to ensure that each guest has enough time but, at the same time, that everyone has his or her turn within the event's hour and half.

At the end of these "introductions," guests will be so comfortable with each other that you won't need to worry about continuing the conversation—they'll continue naturally.

Ten to Fourteen

You use a similar format as above, but you will have to keep a timer on each person, unless everyone is okay with a six-hour dinner (this has happened!). If you are going to have these many people, you need to pay attention to the logistics. Can people see each other? Can they hear each other? Does it still feel like a small gathering? A large round table is the only way to be effective and ensure that every guest is comfortable.

Fourteen Plus

If you are organizing such a large event, your guests need to know each other—at least a little—or it's going to be an ineffective lunch or dinner. While it's tempting to think that you can do more by having more, when it comes to lunches and dinners they should be maxed out at 12 people.

WHO PAYS?

What a great question! Here's something that probably sounds crazy: I spent about $30,000 on lunches and dinners until I stopped paying for every single meal of every single person. Now I pay on occasion, depending on my relationships with those I've invited as well as the vibe of the group and any other factors. For instance, a few months ago, I paid the entire lunch bill because I had to leave early for a flight. The cost of everyone's lunch was well worth the favourable impression I left behind as I ran to catch my plane.

But really, it depends. Let's explore the pros and cons.

If you are bringing people together, I doubt that your guests expects you to pay for their meal. However ... if I'm at a table with people who charge anywhere from $100 to $1,000 an hour, why are they going to give me that time for free?

And let's be honest—paying for lunch or dinner creates a level of respect for you from your guests. It shows that you respect their time and their willingness to spend a chunk of time with you and a bunch of strangers. That's a big request for more than a few people.

"...IT'S ALL ABOUT FAMILIARITY."

So, while I think it's a worthwhile way to show others respect and gratitude, why don't I pay anymore? It's simple: it's all about familiarity. There's a certain point at which your dinners and lunches are no longer with strangers but with second and third connections from people you already know. When you are introduced, social currency is transferred and you don't have to prove your reputation.

I don't have a solution. Some people are insulted if you don't pay; others may not afford the meal. It's up to you, your particular situation, and how comfortable you are with your decision.

MAKING THOSE CONNECTIONS COUNT

The lunch or dinner went well—great! Now it's time to relax.

Just kidding, again.

You know, you can get everything perfect up to this point, but if you don't follow up you'll miss out. Big time.

The guests at these lunches and dinners usually leave on an emotional high. They're excited. They feel empowered. They're ready to take on the world.

But that feeling diminishes quickly. You want to capitalize on the great time they've had as soon as you can in order to continue the conversation and foster as many relationships as possible. You need an actionable follow-up.

"YOU WANT TO CAPITALIZE ON THE GREAT TIME THEY'VE HAD AS SOON AS YOU CAN..."

I follow up with every guest with two emails. The first is an individual email with a specific point, resource, or comment resulting from the dinner. The message here is that our relationship is mutually beneficial—and that I was seriously listening to and contemplating what they said during the meal. The second email goes to everyone. I carbon copy each guest, thank them for their participation, and then remind them that everyone's contact information is enclosed in the email. I usually let the email thread work itself out.

GROWING

The follow-ups have been done, you're interacting with new people as a result of the lunch or dinner, and you're happy. Now what?

There are always two options to success: you can rest on your laurels or keep kicking butt and taking names. I choose to forget the laurels. I can rest when I'm dead.

"I CHOOSE TO FORGET THE LAURELS."

A few things can be done to grow your connections, influence, and successes when it comes to lunches and dinners. Here are my suggestions—but be creative and find what works for you and your communication style.

Between media, social media, news and news feeds it is way too easy to become insular in your experience and thinking. Scotts meals ensure you are challenged and grown as a person, even if he does eat too much steak.

Jeremy Wright

KEEP PLANNING DINNERS

Once you have had a successful lunch or dinner, begin planning the next one. I've done these meals all over the place. I plan them while I'm travelling for business as well as when I'm travelling for pleasure. I also have had multiple dinners in my hometown. These are almost more beneficial than dinners in a place I've never been before: you can rely on your connections to introduce you to more people.

It's also worthwhile—not to mention fun—to re-invite people. Doing so builds community and relationships. It makes your dinners more interesting and offers guests the chance to widen their circles and connections. It can lead to entrepreneurial magic—as people become more comfortable with each other, they're more willing to share and become vulnerable, and, in turn, create the perfect atmosphere to foster problem-solving, collaboration, and dreaming.

"DOING SO BUILDS COMMUNITY AND RELATIONSHIPS."

TAKE TO THE INTERNET

Create a community with a Facebook group or an email thread so that people can keep up with each other. Remember: the dinner or lunch is only the beginning of the conversation. What takes place after can be revolutionary and spectacular—but only if guests keep in touch with each other.

REFLECT

Be critical of your process and give yourself a little constructive criticism. With every dinner and lunch you plan and execute, you'll find better ways of organizing and holding them. Don't be afraid to experiment to see what works for your process.

GOING FROM HERE

It's time to get started! There's nothing more frustrating than having a great idea but not working on it right away. To help, I'm adding a bunch of downloadable documents you can use to plan your own lunch or dinner to foster your own connections that matter. You'll find email templates, questions to ask, and other resources that will make planning and executing your meal a lot simpler. (Why reinvent the wheel, right?)

"THIS ISN'T THE END OF THE CONVERSATION; IT'S THE BEGINNING."

This isn't the end of the conversation; it's the beginning. If you're interested in becoming a connecting force to be reckoned with, you might be interested in joining our exclusive Limitless Mastermind Facebook group. Send me an email and let me know how you'll provide value to the group's members—and what you're hoping to gain in return.

I would love to hear how the experience was for you. Buying this book and completing a lunch or dinner is a leap of faith, but it means even more that you did it. I want to hear from you: how it worked, what you changed, how you would do it differently. Email me at *bonus@theconnectionbook.com*

QUESTIONS AND ANSWERS

In writing this book, I've done research and had conversations with some amazing and brilliant people. It has allowed me to answer your questions.

As I receive more questions, you'll see them on the Connections that Count website. If you have a question, reach out via the website—I'll personally answer it for you!

Q: How do you talk about how the bill will be paid?

First of all, you need to decide if you will take care of the bill or if you would like your guests to pay their own tabs. This is up to you and your level of comfort with your guests. Try to gauge their expectations beforehand and determine if you will pay or leave it to them.

If you plan to take care of the bill, let the host or your server know before your guests arrive. This way, the bill will not be brought to the table and you can discreetly pay for it later without having to discuss it in front of your guests.

If you wish to have your guests pay for their own meals, let the server bring the bills to the table. This usually spurs guests to pay their own meal costs.

Q: What is the best table format?

The best table formats allow each guest to be within comfortable speaking distance of every other guest. For groups of 10 or fewer, this is best accomplished at a standard round or rectangular table. Do not use place cards for seating unless you have strong feelings about certain guests sitting next to each other because it will benefit them. Otherwise, allow guests to sit as they please.

For larger groups (10+) seat your guests at multiple smaller tables. A

Scott has a talent to get colleagues thinking not just about work but abou life and the integral balance between booth. Very thankful for his inspiring push to have us connect "live" in a very digital world!

Karen Moores

guest at one end of a table for 30 cannot chat with someone at the other end of that table, and it's impossible to maintain stimulating conversation among that many people. Smaller tables ensure that guests are comfortable talking among themselves and make it easier (and faster) for the restaurant staff to serve them.

Q: What's the difference between a private room and a typical placement?

A private room is private. You can close the door and your guests are the only people in that room. The benefit of renting a private room is that it's quiet and your guests are more likely to generate conversation because they're not worried about being overheard by the other diners in the room. The cons of private rooms are that the serving staff cannot serve your guests as discreetly as they normally would (the act of opening a door and entering a room interrupts a conversation, no matter what) and some restaurants require a fee or a minimum number of guests to secure a private room.

If you're not dining privately, a typical placement would be a reserved table in a restaurant's regular dining area. Many restaurants can accommodate a request for a table in a quiet location and not in the mainstream of restaurant traffic. Servers can easily get to and from your table discreetly without having to interrupt the conversation. However, you will be in earshot of other diners and this may impede the openness of the conversation you hope to have.

Q: How do I ensure that the first 20 minutes aren't awkward?

Do not count on your guests to immediately jump into a conversation with each other. The first 20 minutes need to be nurtured by you. Start by talking about yourself and sharing the type of stories and information you hope your guests will later share. Keep it short—you don't want to be the host who spends the entire event talking about him- or herself. After this, ask questions of your guests to get the conversation flowing. When you ask questions, be prepared to share your own answers if the conversation lags among your guests. After these initial questions, stop providing your input and instead prompt guests with more questions as they become more comfortable with each other.

Q: How do I keep the conversation going and ensure that each person has time to talk?

Do the math. Consider the number of people at the table and how long you expect to be there. Do not assign specific speaking times to each guest but be wary of approximately how long each guest has to speak. When a guest has monopolized the conversation, look for segues to move the conversation to another guest. It's best to interject by asking a question or redirecting the conversation to a specific person, not opening it up for a general response, because that guest will likely resume his or her monologue.

Q: How do I plan for and keep track of the length of the lunch or dinner?

Above all, be respectful of your guests' schedules. For lunches, most will have to be back at the office for the afternoon and cannot linger. For dinners, many will want to get home to family.

Begin the meal by asking guests if there are hard stop times which you need to consider. If anyone indicates a time by which they must leave, bring that person into the conversation early and ensure that he or she has a fair opportunity to talk and share. As the hard stop time approaches, ask that guest if he or she wants to add anything before leaving. Do not guilt guests into staying longer than they are able—this experience is about being comfortable, open, and honest.

If the end time has been set by you, let your guests know when the event will wrap up, and monitor the conversation so that you have time to cover all the topics you had planned.

If you find yourself dining with a group with no time constraints, take advantage of this. Rarely is anyone able to allocate unlimited time to spend with strangers, but when this happens it leads to amazing results. Let conversation happen organically once guests are comfortable steering the direction of things. Only interject if one person is taking up too much of the group's time; otherwise, let the subject matter change organically and don't feel obliged to stick to the set list of topics you've prepared.

Q: Is there anything that the restaurant needs to know in advance?

If you're expecting a variance of more than two people from the original reservation, let the restaurant know as soon as possible. Tell them that you're hosting a business meeting and would like a quiet table or private room, depending on your group's needs. The restaurant also needs to know of guests' dietary restrictions or severe allergies. Otherwise, these lunches and dinners follow a standard procedure in restaurants and, if your reservation is accurate, the restaurant does not need any special instruction.

Q: Do you order any specific drinks or wine for lunch or dinner?

The only liberty you should ever take in ordering on behalf of your guests is water for the table. Otherwise, your guests order individually what they prefer. The same applies for you order what you typically order when you dine out. If you're a soda drinker, order soda—not a fancy cocktail just to impress your guests.

Q: What happens if people cancel at the last minute?

If multiple people cancel at the last minute, you may need to reschedule the event itself. If you feel there are still enough guests to make the lunch or dinner a success, proceed with those who can make it. You can also bump up the number of guests by extending some warm invites to people you know who might be willing to add a last-minute event to their schedule. Remember, even though you know that last-minute person, others at the table likely don't, and introductions are necessary.

When guests provide you with a legitimate reason for their last-minute cancellation, be understanding and try to rebook them at a later date.

When guests simply do not show up or offer no reason for cancelling, those guests were not a good fit for the event. Do not offer to reschedule those guests for another event.

Q: What can you do to foster a follow-up at the end of a lunch or dinner?

Before the meal ends, ask guests if they would like to be connected with each other via email. They usually do, and you can follow up with one email. Send an email with every guest carbon copied, thanking them for attending and encouraging them to follow up with one another.

If you know of individual guests who have action items to discuss, connect those people personally with an individual, more personal email. Remember that the point of the meal is not only to connect the guests but also to make your own connections! Reach out to every guest with individual emails following the event, adding personal details about why you valued meeting that person. Add guests' names to your social networks and create an email list so that everyone can stay connected.

Q: What's the worst thing that has happened at a lunch or dinner?

One of the bigger fires I've had to put out was when a guest began doing illegal drugs at dinner. Let's hope that was a one-time thing! Lots of little things can go wrong; it's important to remain level-headed and deal with them the best way you can.

You can learn from my errors. Once I didn't make a reservation; when I arrived at the venue, they couldn't accommodate my party. I've made the mistake of not socially proofing my guests; this resulted in a mixture of people who did not enjoy each other's company. Finally, many people cancelled at the last minute or didn't show up because I failed to follow up properly in the days leading to the event.

Q: What's the best thing that's happened at a lunch or dinner?

Dinners with no time limit lead guests to generate the best conversations. I've sat at a table with strangers and left six hours later with some of my best friends. Many of these people are now in business with me and/or other dinner guests. The single biggest deal I've witnessed at a lunch was a handshake for $250,000 in funding. In addition to the monetary value, another major benefit is seeing people allow their authentic selves to shine through.

Q: Does this only work for business folks or anyone in any field?

Anyone in any field can make this work. In fact, this method of connecting likely works better with non-business fields, where the concept of networking doesn't have such a strong presence. You won't need to break down preexisting notions of networking.

Q: Can you introduce me to someone who would plan it with me?

Absolutely. Get in touch with me, let me know which city you plan to host in, and I'll see what I can do! :)

Q: Would you come to a lunch or dinner that I host?

I would LOVE to. I travel frequently and, any time I do, I organize and attend lunches and dinners. If I came to your city and you hosted the lunch or dinner instead of me—well, that would be wonderful.

Q: What do you tip after these lunches and dinners?

It is common for restaurants to automatically add gratuity to the bill for larger groups. This is a policy over which the wait staff has no control, so if you have an issue with paying the full amount of gratuity that has been added to your bill, go directly to the restaurant manager.

If the service and food were excellent, tip generously and let the staff know you appreciated their hard work. If this is a venue you plan to use regularly, let the manager know that the excellence of

"We all know connections are invaluable in business. But how do you meet and build relationships with the right people? Scott Oldford's step-by-step guide shows that anything is possible and anyone is reachable with the right intention and planning. You'll soon be connecting and collaborating with the best in your field."

Dorie Clark, *author of* Reinventing You *and adjunct professor, Duke University Fuqua School of Business*

their service has earned them return customers. They'll recognize you when you return and you'll reap the benefits of being a repeat customer.

If the service and food were not up to par, tip at a minimum. Speak to your server or a manager about what went wrong or where you expected it to be better, and let them know you were disappointed.

Q: Can you expense lunches and dinners?

Yes. Your specific accounting practices will determine whether you can consider these to be personal or company expenses—typically they're considered business. Be sure to keep receipts and document properly.

Q: What venues do you enjoy the most for lunches/dinners? Which work better than others?

I like using any venue that offers a private room, and I stay away from public places that are mostly open spaces with little privacy for conversation. I like using mid-range to slightly high-end restaurants, avoiding pub-style chain restaurants and expensive posh restaurants. Read online reviews to find venues known for their great service—this affects the smoothness of your event. I tend to host at steakhouses, as they consistently hit all the key things I look for: great service, quality food at a reasonable price, and privacy.

Q: Do you have suggestions on which days of the week to plan events?

I've found that, for dinners, Tuesdays, Wednesdays, and Thursdays work best. Thursdays and Fridays work best for lunches, as many people like to "wind down" at the end of a week and take a long lunch break.

In the same vein, I've noticed that 7:30 p.m. is the best time to schedule a dinner, with 8 p.m. the latest I'm willing to go. If you

schedule a dinner after 8 p.m., you'll most likely see an uptick in cancellations. The worst time to schedule a dinner is 5:30 p.m.: traffic can be congested and result in late arrivers or cancellations.

LUNCH AND DINNER TOPICS

I upped my game with lunches and dinners when I became intentional about my questions. These questions, replicated from friends and others, allow you to ask questions that most people would never hear.

I ask each person these questions, but typically each question is different and picked for a specific person so that it is both relevant and allows you to strike quickly.

- What are you most afraid to desire?
- Why do you do what you do?
- Where are you most vulnerable?
- What is your deepest shame?
- What do you do that is not socially acceptable?
- What is one experience you've had that you don't believe anyone else has ever experienced?
- What is a belief you'd be willing to die for?
- What would it look like if you peeled away your mask?
- What is the most difficult decision you've ever made?
- If today were the last day of your life, would you do what you're about to do today? If not, what would you do instead?
- What is something you'd happily fail at?
- When do you feel you can surrender yourself completely?
- What worries you most about the future?

- What are you holding on to that you need to let go?
- What is your self-talk like?
- What is the biggest mistake you've ever made?
- Why do you matter?
- Are you happy with yourself?
- When were you most afraid? Heartbroken? Lonely?
- What is something that you pretend to understand when you really don't?

CHECKLIST

You're all ready to go! Here is the list that you will want to take with you. You can download it from the resources section of the Connections that Count website.

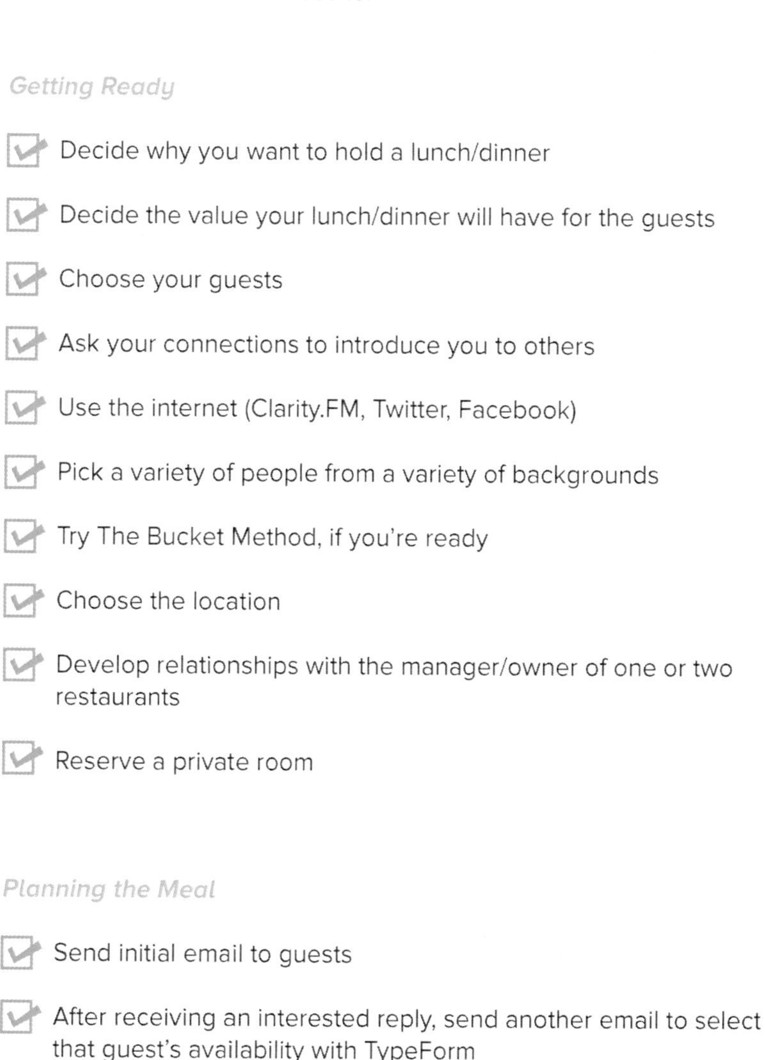

Getting Ready

- ☑ Decide why you want to hold a lunch/dinner
- ☑ Decide the value your lunch/dinner will have for the guests
- ☑ Choose your guests
- ☑ Ask your connections to introduce you to others
- ☑ Use the internet (Clarity.FM, Twitter, Facebook)
- ☑ Pick a variety of people from a variety of backgrounds
- ☑ Try The Bucket Method, if you're ready
- ☑ Choose the location
- ☑ Develop relationships with the manager/owner of one or two restaurants
- ☑ Reserve a private room

Planning the Meal

- ☑ Send initial email to guests
- ☑ After receiving an interested reply, send another email to select that guest's availability with TypeForm

While I might opt occasionally for hosting home dinners cause I love to cook, Scott Oldford's A to Z "connection dining playbook" demonstrates very well how building your social connections strategically is so valuable for your business. For your lifestyle. Especially in a trusted, curated rather intimate environment - around a hosted dining table.

If you are a future minded achiever, and you are looking for THE way to progress your lifestyle and business to your next level. Setting up your own dinners- wherever you are- could be the most effective (and fun!) approach forward. This book shows you the way.

David Brower, High Performance Living,
The Sensorial Guy

- [x] After date/time confirmation from all guests, transfer the information from TypeForm to Excel

- [x] Sort people by profession and biggest challenges to spur conversation/introductions

- [x] Follow up with a confirmation of the lunch/dinner date, time, and venue with Contactually

- [x] Include email address (Fancy Hands) that guests are to use if they are delayed or need to cancel

- [x] Add all confirmed guests to a Google Calendar invite, set to "private"

- [x] Send out reminders from Contactually
    - Three days before
    - One day before
    - The morning of

- [x] Use Fancy Hands to take care of cancellations, delays, and changes

During the Meal

- [x] Make small talk while guests arrive

- [x] Guide discussion during ordering toward actually ordering

- [x] After the order has been taken, introduce yourself, thank everyone for coming, explain the format of the meal
    - Begin introductions with one person
    - Who they are, what they're passionate about
    - What keeps them awake at night or greatest challenge and how it can be solved
    - Random question for the table

After the Meal

- [x] Send a personal email to every guest
    - Specific point, resource, or comment from dinner

- [x] Send a group email
    - Carbon copy everyone, thank them for participating, and note that everyone's contact information is included in the email

- [x] Begin planning the next dinner

- [x] Create a community with a Facebook group or through an email thread

- [x] Reflect on your process and make changes as needed

If you're ready to get serious about planning your first meal, head over to theconnectionbook.com/resources to download electronic copies of these checklists. You can print them out, mark them up, and make copies for each dinner you host.

EMAIL TEMPLATES

The email templates below haven't been used just by me but they have allowed me to bring people together across the world.

However, use them as templates—guidelines. You'll want your own personality to come through. If your tone is humorous, serious, or somewhere in between, ensure that you are quick-and-to-the-point and leave a little social proof so that those reading it understand how the meal can benefit them.

Asking for a Connection

Hi [NAME]!

I hope you're doing well! I'm sending a quick email to ask you for a favour. I was hoping that you might be able to put me in touch with [NAME] because [REASON]. If you could introduce me to [NAME], I'd be grateful—and owe you one!

I'm really hoping that I can include them in a {insert type} that I'm holding later this month and would appreciate the connection.

In the meantime, I would love to catch up. Is there anything I can help you with at this moment?

Know that I appreciate and enjoy your presence, you mean the world to me!

Thanks,

Scott

Asking someone to set up a lunch or dinner

Hi [NAME]!

I'll be in [CITY] on [DATE] and was wondering if you could help me by planning a [LUNCH/DINNER]. I like to plan meals with new people whenever I travel so that I can meet and connect with brilliant folks wherever I am. Since you know [CITY] better than I do, I've got my fingers crossed that you'll help me plan an awesome [LUNCH/DINNER].

I was hoping that we could set up 20 minutes to talk later this week; does {date and time} work for you? If so, I'll send you the skype details and we'll take it from there!

Let me know!

Talk soon,

Scott

Asking a Stranger

[NAME],

Hope all is going well!

I want to invite you to a [LUNCH/DINNER] on [DATE]. I love meeting and connecting with new people. Recently, I have been bringing strangers together, both here in [LOCATION] and across North America. You can expect engaging conversation and a great time—which I know you'll enjoy.

I've borrowed the concept from a great friend of mine, Scott Oldford, from his new book *Connections that Count.* If you haven't checked it out, it's a great concept and I'd LOVE to have you there.

If you're up for it, I'm hosting it on {information}. If the specific date and time doesn't work, I do these on a fairly regular basis, so I'm certain we can make something work. :)

Hope to hear from you soon!

Asking Someone You Know

Hey [NAME],

I'm putting together a few lunches and dinners this month and would love to have you there! Are you free for lunch on [DATE]? I'm really excited to bring awesome people together for interesting conversations.

If you're up for it, let me know. If the specific date and time doesn't work, I do these on a regular basis, so I'm certain we can make something work :).

Hope to hear from you soon!

Scott

Confirming Lunch/Dinner

[NAME]

I'm really looking forward to having lunch with you next week! I've made a reservation for [DATE] [TIME] at [PLACE]. I'd appreciate it if you can confirm that you'll be there.

Thanks,

Scott

Simplicity is the ultimate form of sophistication. Scott brought up a simple yet powerful way to rescue meaning in your contacts, your business, and who knows, your life. The book goes smoothly from the bird's eye view on how to create true connections down to details on how to balance invitee's backgrounds, deal with availability, follow-ups, making the "big day" happen and so on. Grab your copy of the book, and dare to connect, to reach out people meaningfully, to build true relationships. Money is the shadow, real connections are life. Start building them, 'Connections that Count' can show you how.

Joao Reis

Confirming Lunch/Dinner (day before)

Hey [NAME],

Just want to confirm that all is good for our lunch tomorrow. I'll see you at [TIME] at [PLACE]!

Thanks,

Scott

Email after Rejection

[NAME],

It's unfortunate you won't be attending the lunch. I think you would have brought a lot of value to the table, and I would have loved to have introduced you to [PERSON].

I organize these [LUNCHES/DINNERS] fairly often, so if you're ever interested in attending another, let me know! I'd be thrilled to have you there.

Thanks,

Scott

Email after Confirmation

[NAME],

Thanks for confirming! I'm really looking forward to getting together with you. If there's anything specific you want to talk about or anything else I should be aware of before we meet, let me know. I try to keep these as free-flowing yet meaningful as possible, and preparation is key!

See you soon,

Scott

Email for more Information

Hi [NAME],

Great to hear you're interested in [LUNCH/DINNER] on [DATE]. I realize it's a different concept so here are a few pointers to ensure that you know what you're getting into. :)

[ITEMS MORE INFORMATION IS NEEDED ON]

Really hope you can make it!

Thanks,

Scott

Email to Follow Up (no reply) #1

Hi [NAME],

Wanted to quickly follow up on my last email inviting you to [LUNCH/DINNER] on [DATE]. I hope you can join us and that you'll love the brilliant conversation.

I need to confirm the number of guests by [DATE], so please respond as soon as you can to let me know if you'll be joining us.

Thanks,

Scott

Email to Follow Up (no reply) #2

[NAME],

I hope all is well. I haven't heard from you if you'll be attending [LUNCH/DINNER] on [DATE]. If you will be joining us, please respond to let me know. I wouldn't want you to show up and not have a seat for you!

If you have any questions, please let me know. If you're unsure about attending, I'd be happy to discuss the benefits of these events with you. I hope to hear back from you!

Thanks,

Scott

Email for When You're in Town

Hi [NAME]!

I'll be in [CITY] on [DATE] and wondered if you could help me in planning a [LUNCH/DINNER]. I love meeting new people whenever I travel.

I've planned [LUNCH/DINNER] for [DATE] at [VENUE]. I've been working on getting some awesome people together, but my connections in [CITY] are limited. Since you know this place much better than I, I hope that you'll join us for [LUNCH/DINNER] and help me bring some great people together. Could you recommend some brilliant minds that I should invite to join us?

Let me know!

Talk soon,

Scott

Email to Ask for Others Who Would Be Interested

Hi [NAME],

It was so cool to meet you at [LUNCH/DINNER]! My brain is still spinning from all the awesome conversation and connections that were made.

If you enjoyed our [LUNCH/DINNER] as much as I did, I hope you'll help me organize another. I'll take care of the details and logistics, but I'm hoping you'll recommend others to invite. If you know of anyone who'd be a good fit for such an event, and would be interested in joining us, could you connect me with them so we can make it happen?

Thanks!

Scott

Email to Follow Up Individually

[NAME],

It was so great meeting you at [LUNCH/DINNER]! I hope you took as much value from it as I did. Wasn't that conversation about [TOPIC] just brilliant? I love getting new perspectives.

If there's anything I can do for you, please reach out. I'm here to help in any way I can, and now that we've met in person I hope you'll be comfortable asking. Whether you want to plan your own [LUNCH/DINNER], need an introduction that I can make, or want to talk business, I'm all ears.

Keep in touch,

Scott

Email to Follow Up to Entire Group

Hi all!

As agreed during [LUNCH/DINNER], I'm sending this email to everyone as a means of distributing everyone's contact information.

It was so great to meet you all—and, more importantly, to have you all meet each other. I hope you all gained as much as I did from our [LUNCH/DINNER]. With so many brilliant minds at one table, it was impossible for that conversation to have gone any way other than amazing! ;)

Now that I've followed up as promised, it's your turn! Reach out to anyone you promised a follow-up to and keep building on what we started.

I'm always here and certainly will be inviting you to other lunches and dinners in the future. :)

Thanks,

Scott

Email to Follow Up to Entire Group (after a Month)

Hi all!

It's hard to believe it's been a month since we had [LUNCH/DINNER] together. But looking back at the last month, it's also hard to believe how much has happened since then. Time is relative, I guess. ;)

I'm following up to see what you've all been up to since we chatted. What's new and exciting? I'd LOVE to hear about the ripple effect of the impact of our meal together.

Here's to keeping in touch!

Scott

Scott breathes new life into an old concept – networking. His straight-forward approach to relationship building is like fresh citrus in an age of brown bananas. Even Jesus knew relationships are best built around food.

Steve Sisler, *Behavioural Profiler and Author of* Eron Prison

BONUSES

If you want to keep up on the latest for resources, the latest copy of the book, and what I've found works best in continuing this journey, register for the latest on the *Connections that Count* website.

If you've purchased this book, email your receipt to *bonus@theconnectionbook.com* and I'll get you access to the private Facebook community, Additional Questions to Spark Authenticity, The Five Secrets to Authentic Connections, exclusive montly Q&A hangouts, and access to Scott (me!) by email.

Thoughts, questions, or just want to reach out? The contact form on the website is the for-sure way to get in touch. :)

THANK YOU

This book came out of having lunches and dinners with amazing people across the world. I want to have lunches and dinners with even more amazing people and know that our secret to success is knowing more and more on a deeper level than just connecting allows.

Although I'm currently researching "connection" further and want to know why two people "click," this book contains everything you need to surround yourself with people that will truly change your life.

I have to thank every single person on my team at INFINITUS, Joanna Guldin-Noll for helping me write this, and Iona Bulgin for teaching me so much about how frequently I use the word brilliant :).

Every person I've surrounded myself with in the past year—thank you. It's been, and continues to be, an amazing journey. Let's make it an amazing next step, shall we?